By Jordan Biggio

As a bonus each classic automobile design is listed twice in this book. Not only does this give you the opportunity to color each scene twice, it also gives you a clean slate in case you make a mistake! It is like having two copies of the same book.

As a second bonus, both the front and back cover are printed with a matte finish. This means you can color them too!

Thank you for purchasing a copy of my book. I had a great time creating this book for you and I would to see what you do with the designs. Feel free to email me images of what you have colored. My email address is:

jordanbiggio@gmail.com

If you enjoyed coloring my designs, then please leave a review to let others know what you thought, be it good or bad. Leaving a review is the single best way to help support me and my art. Leaving a review is easy and don't forget to post a completed colored page with your review.

Thanks again!

Jordan

ISBN-13: 978-1534622401
ISBN-10: 1534622403

FREE BONUS!

Get 5 FREE coloring pages at my website.

www.jordanbiggio.com

A Sample of What's Inside

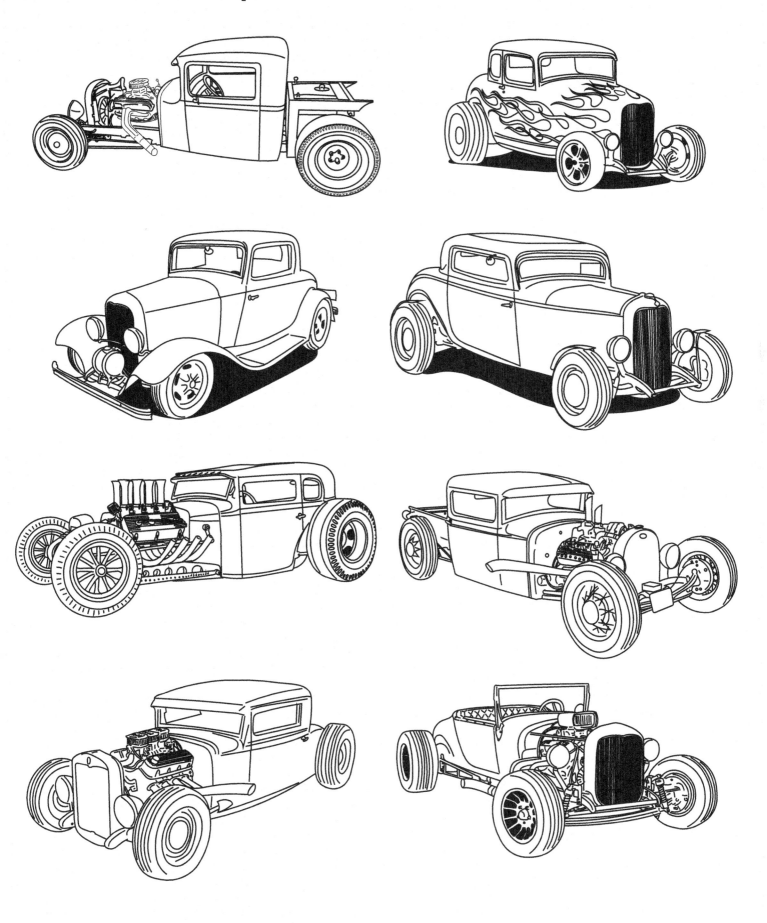

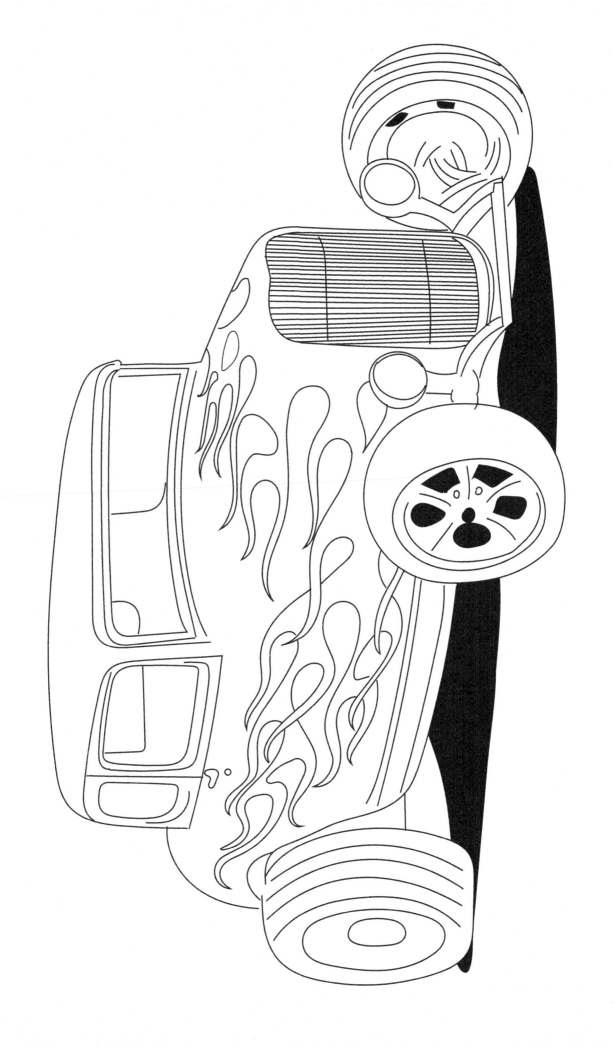

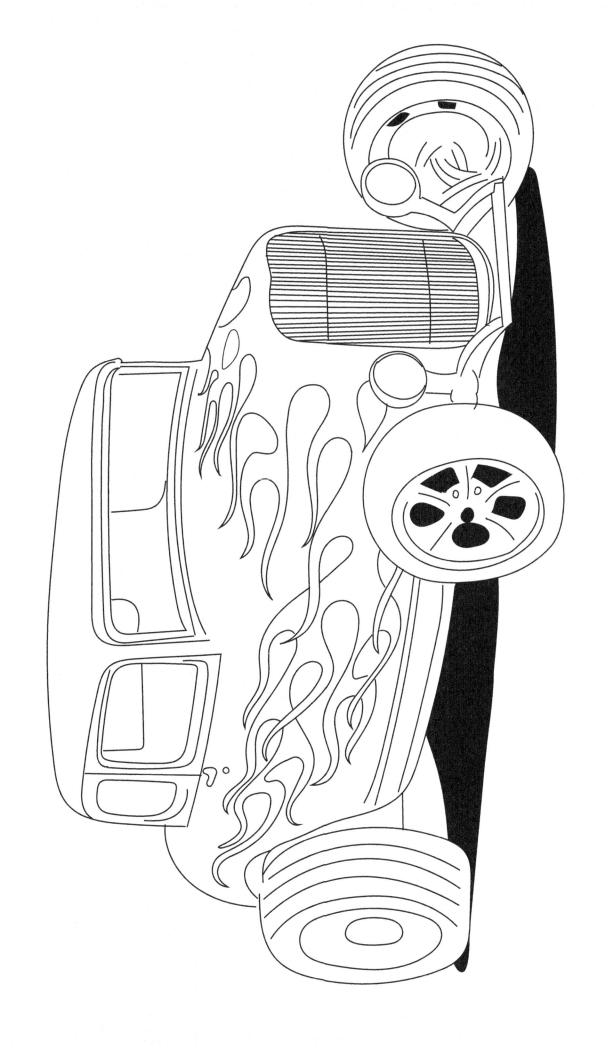

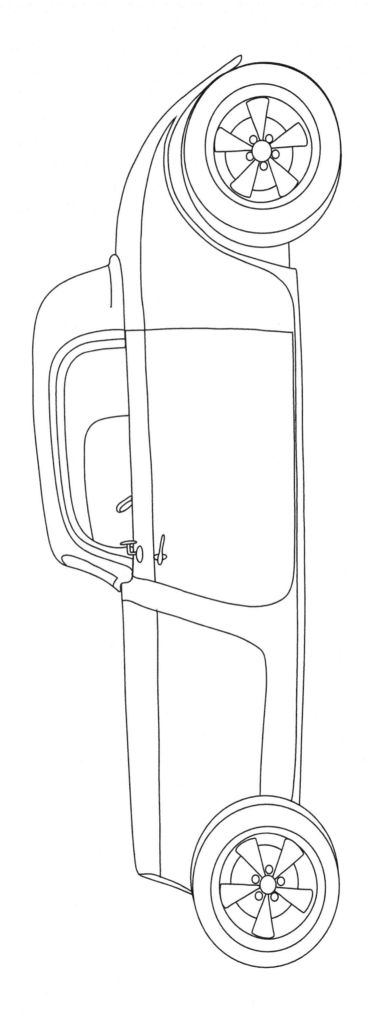

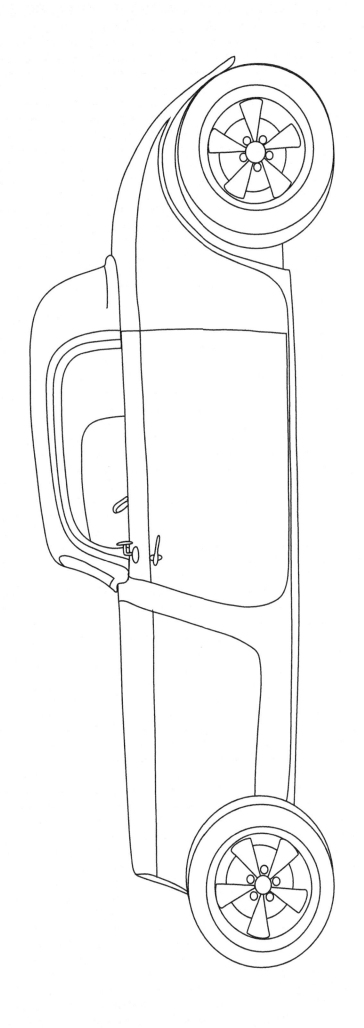

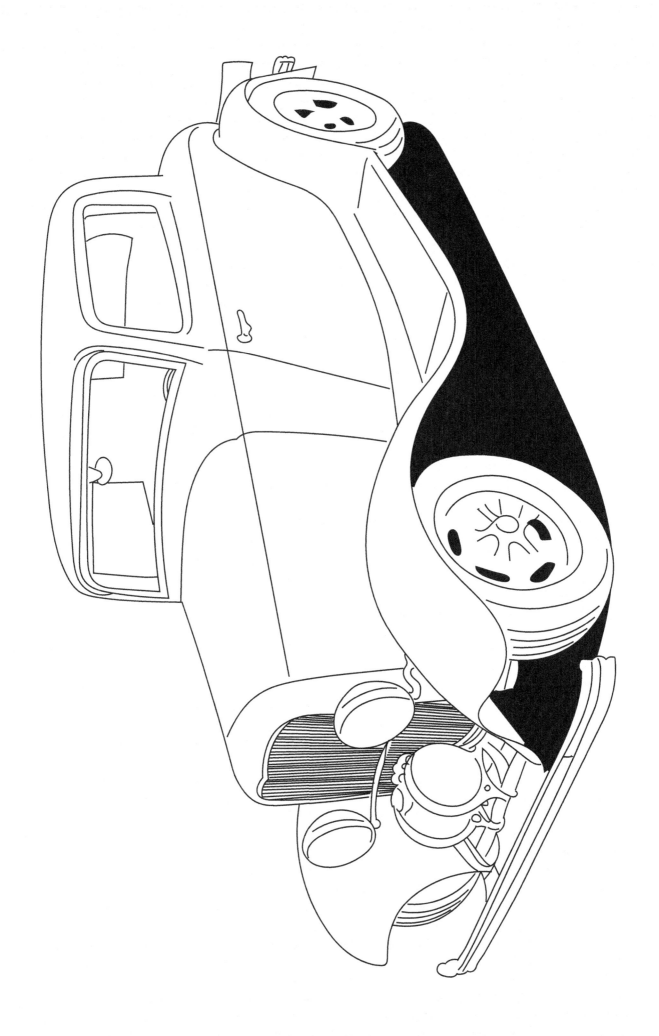

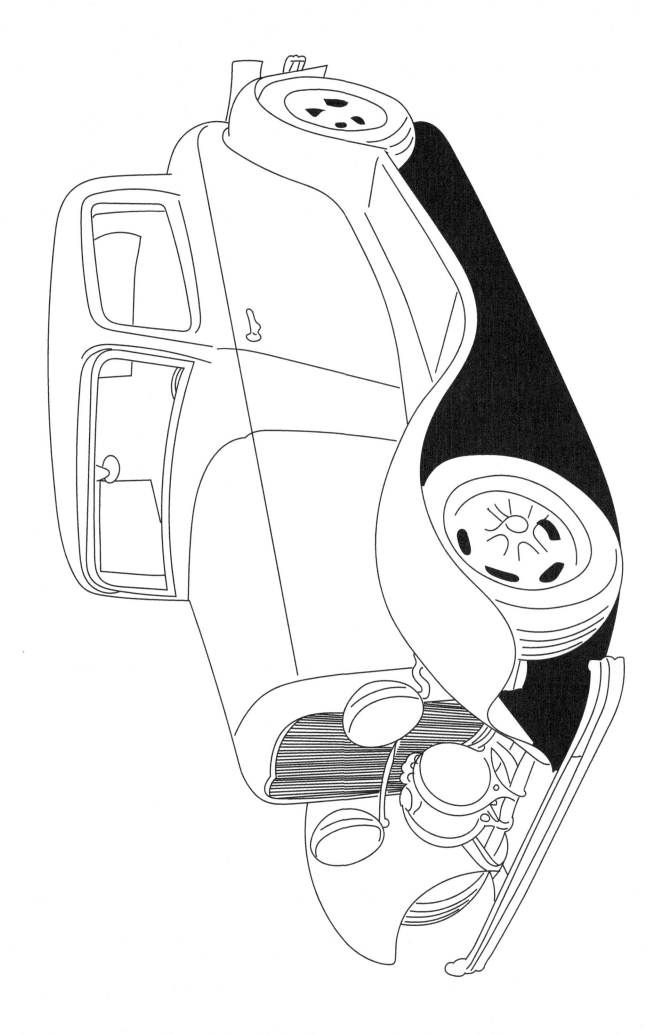

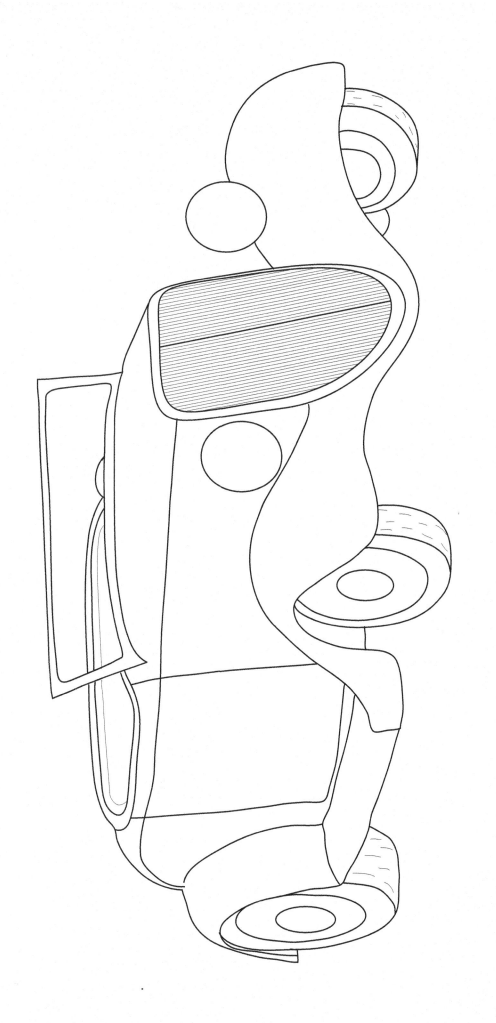

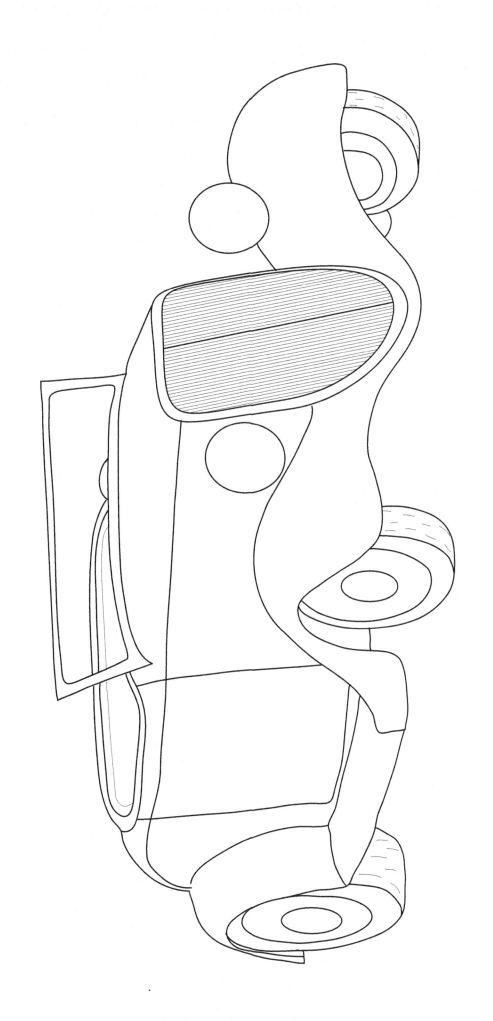

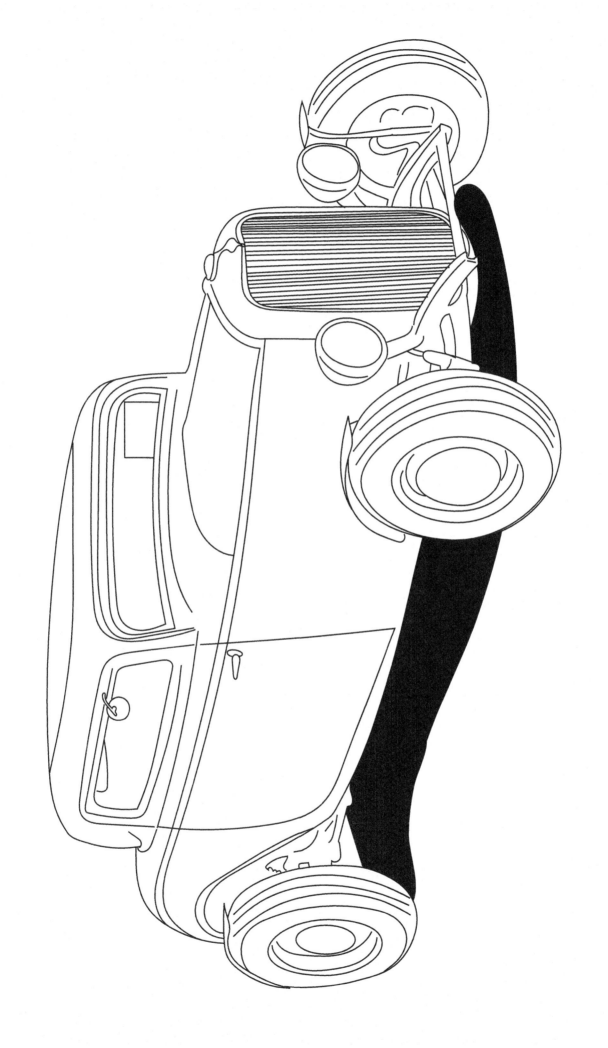

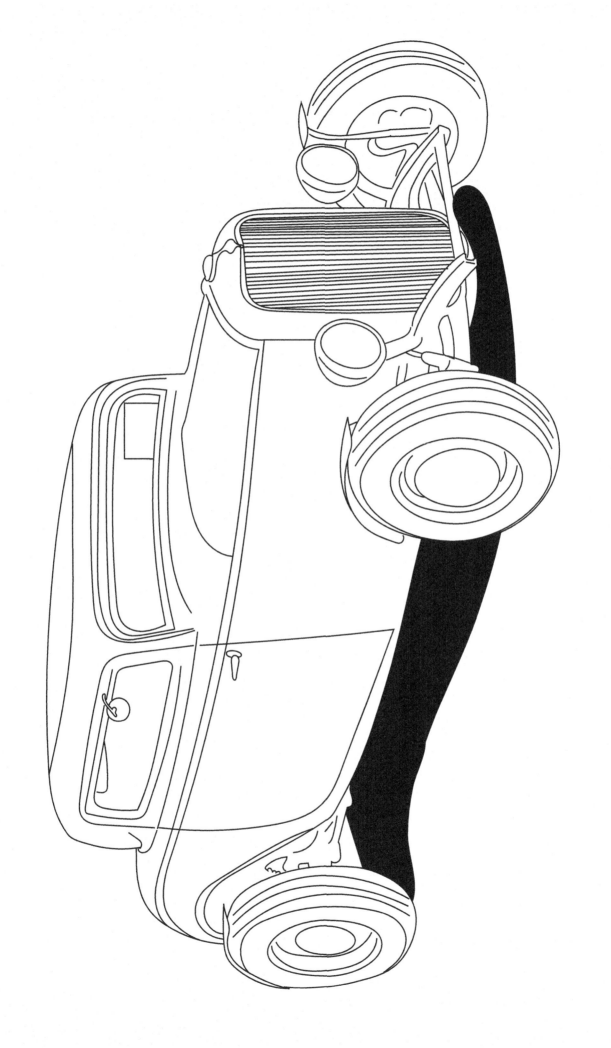

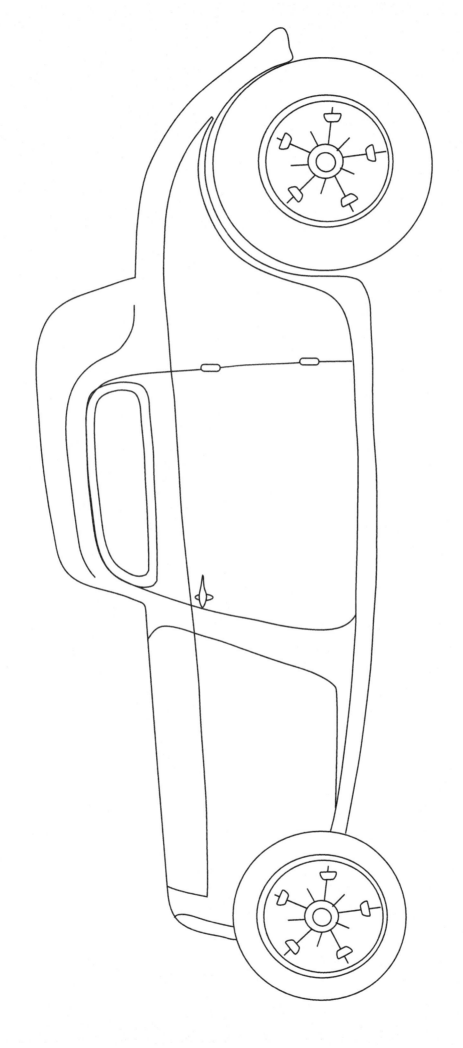

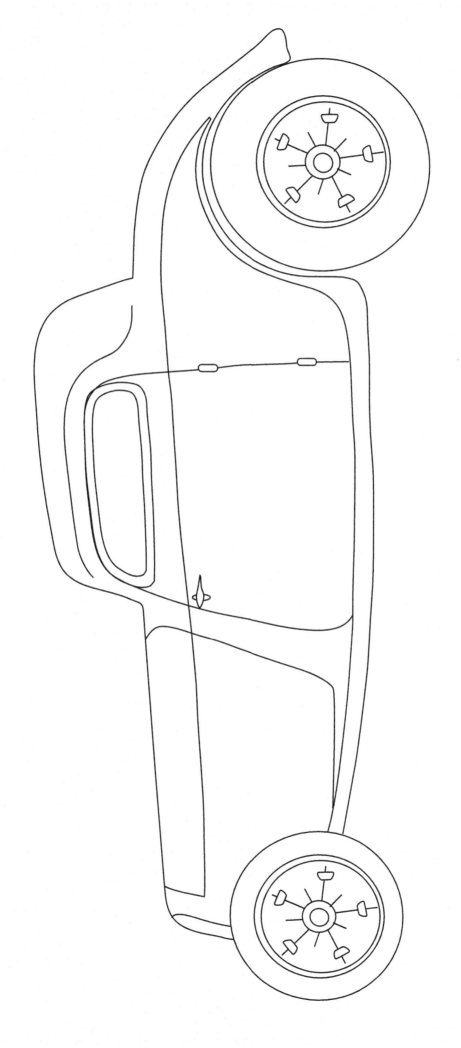

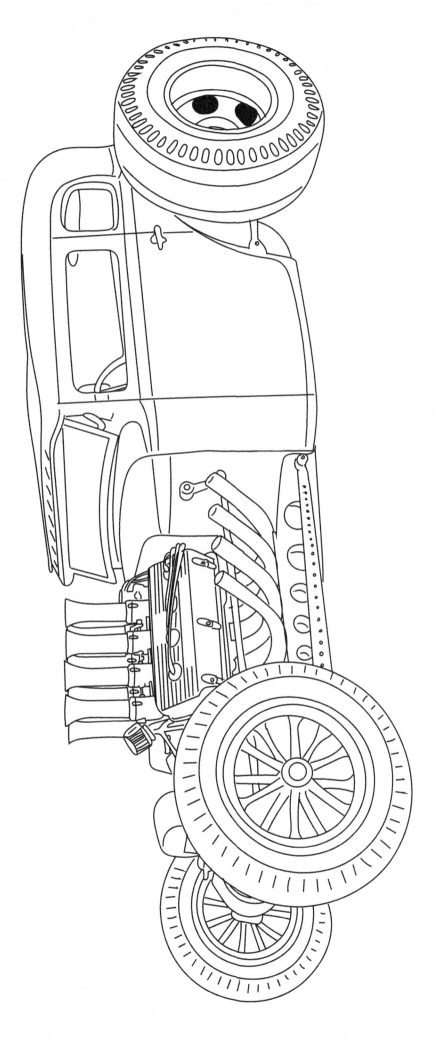

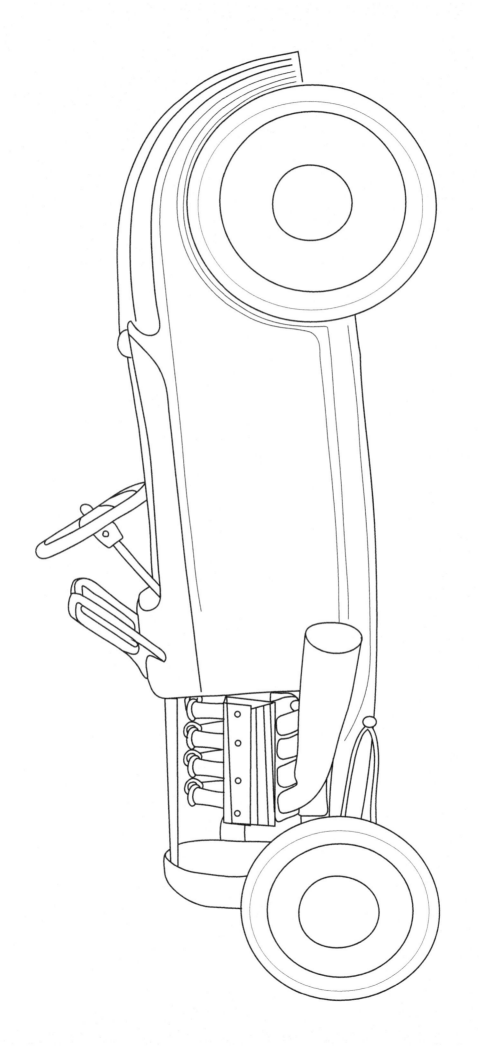

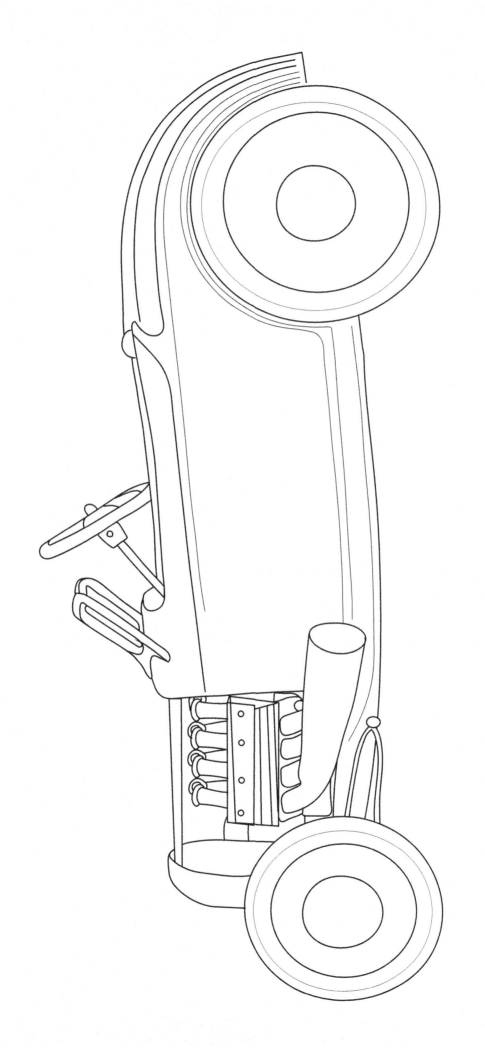

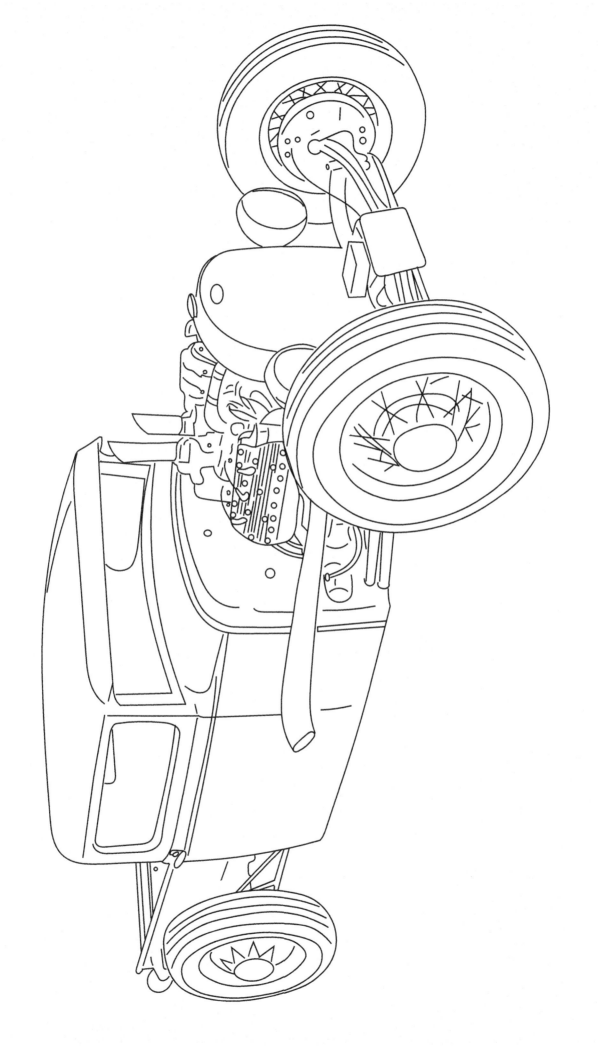

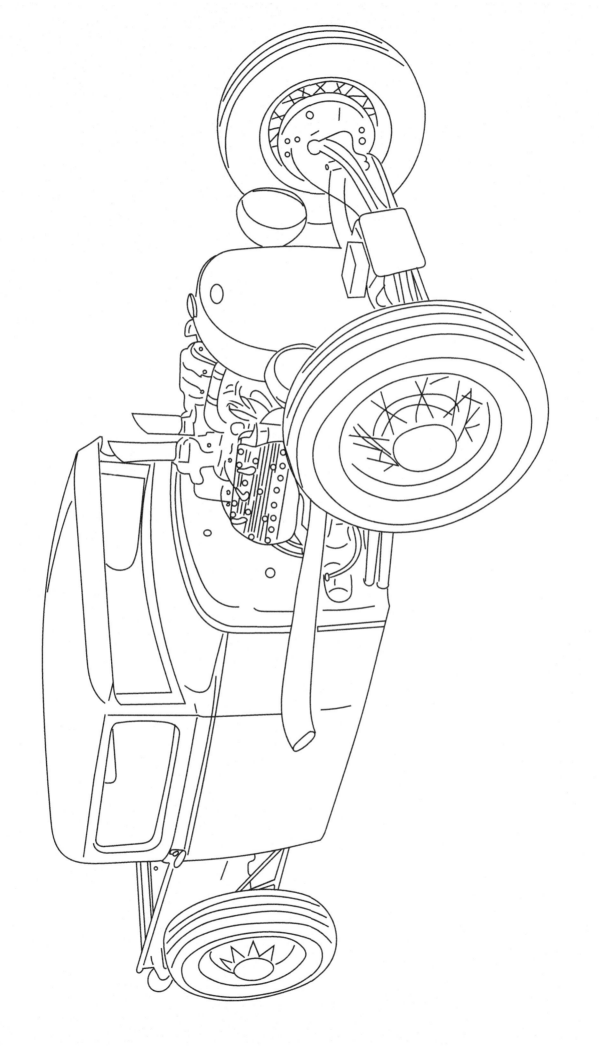

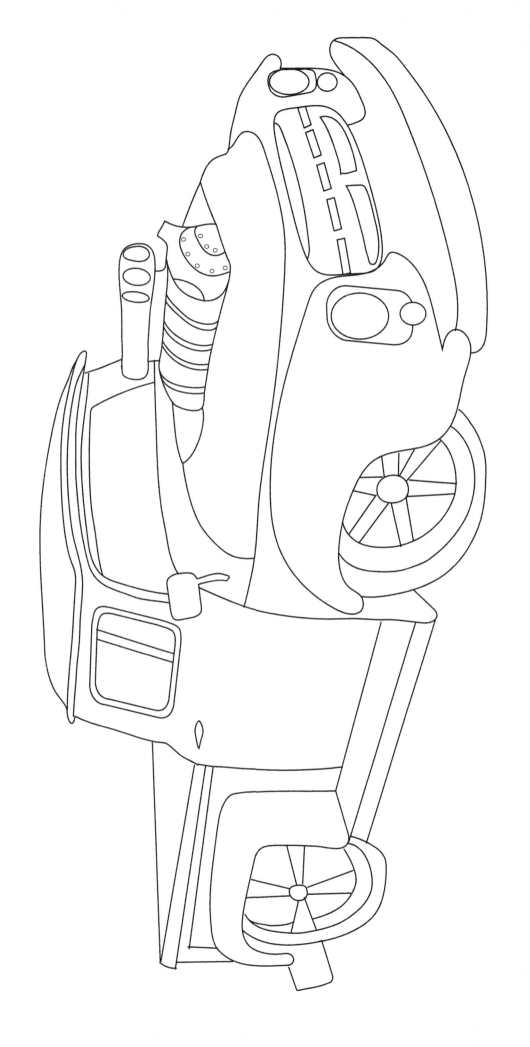

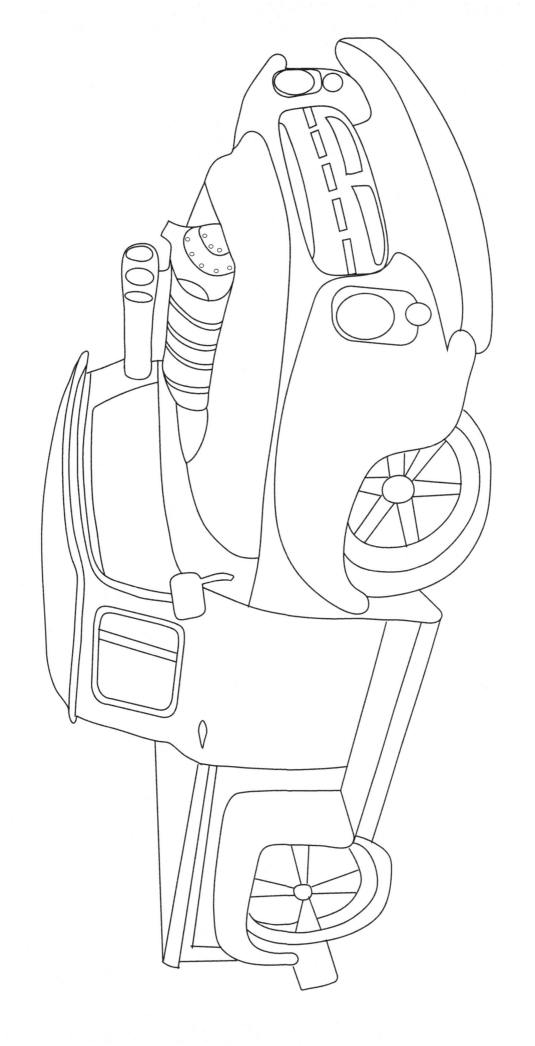

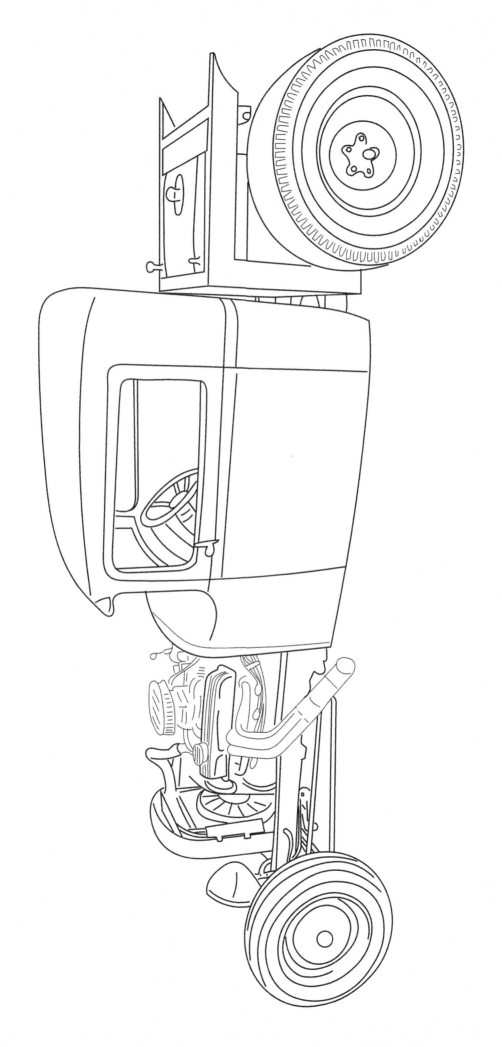

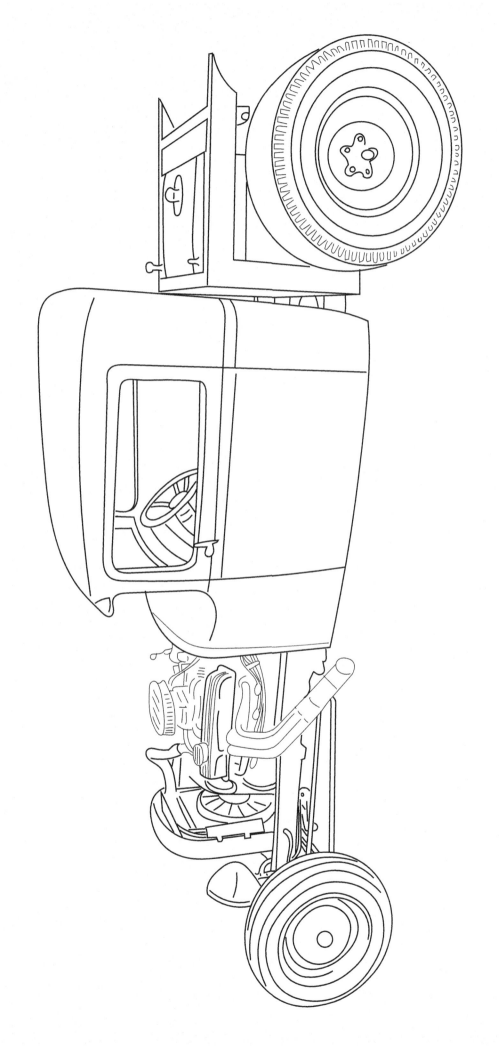

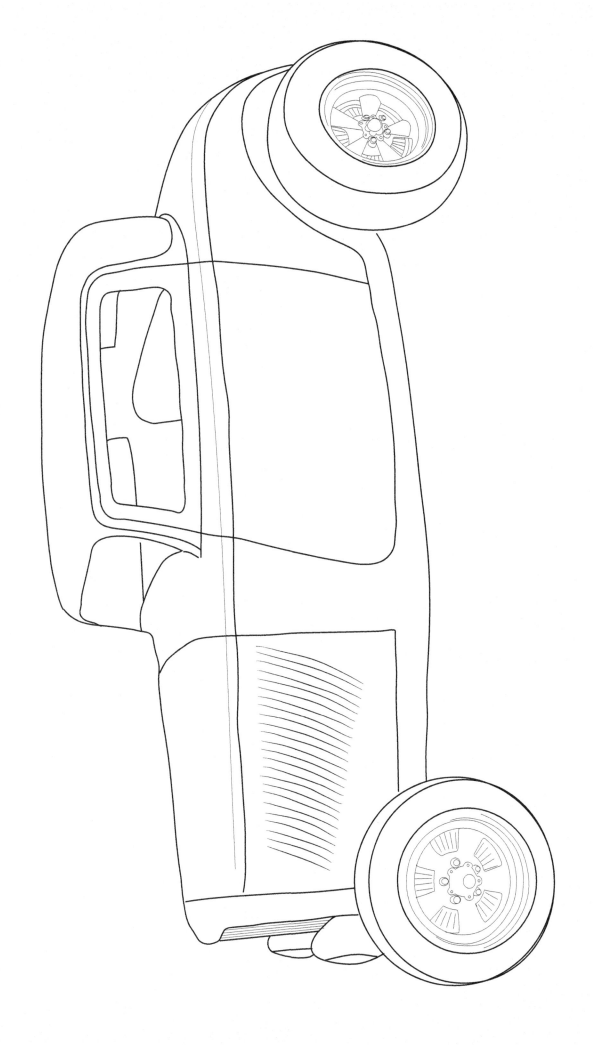

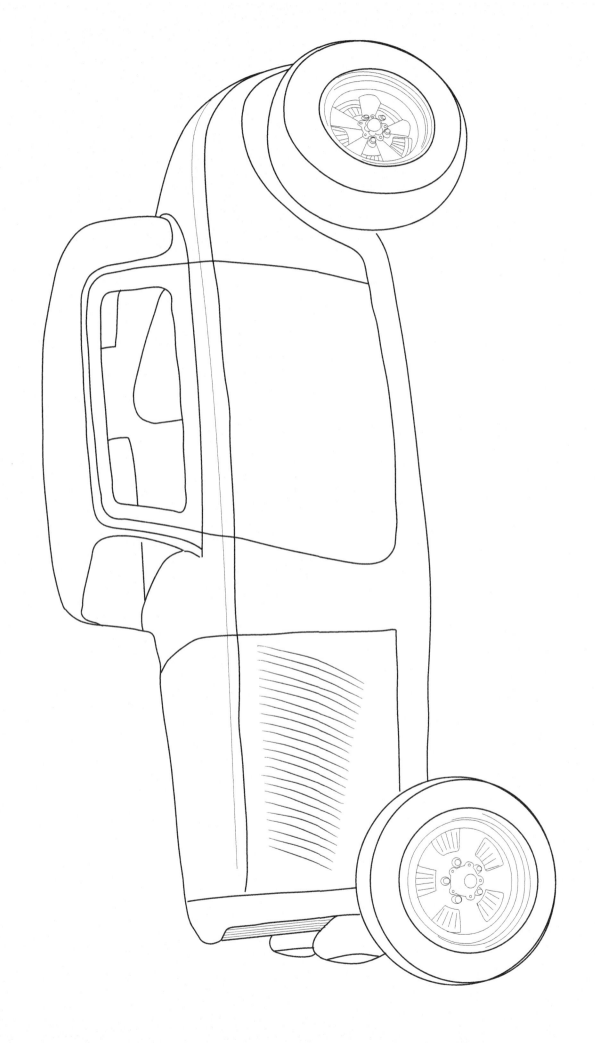

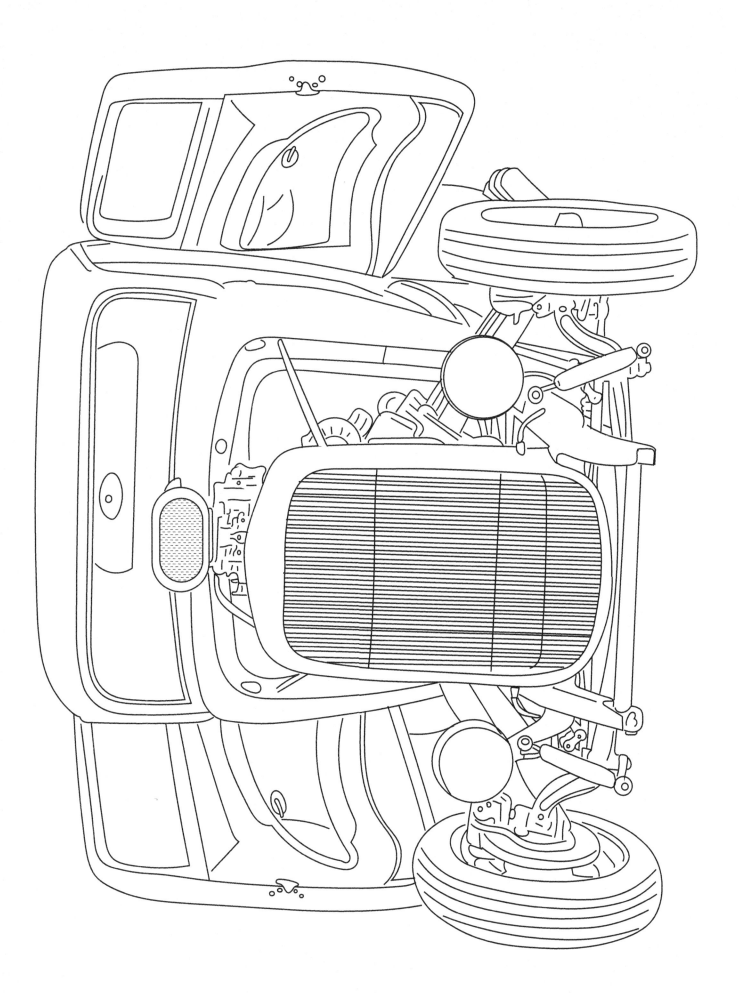

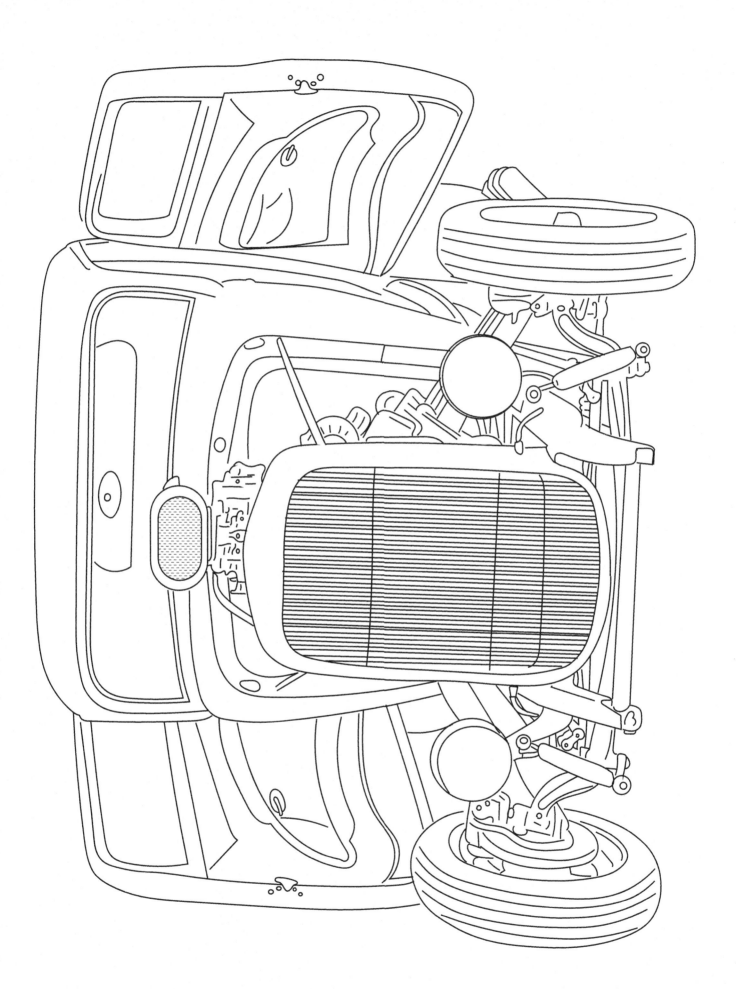

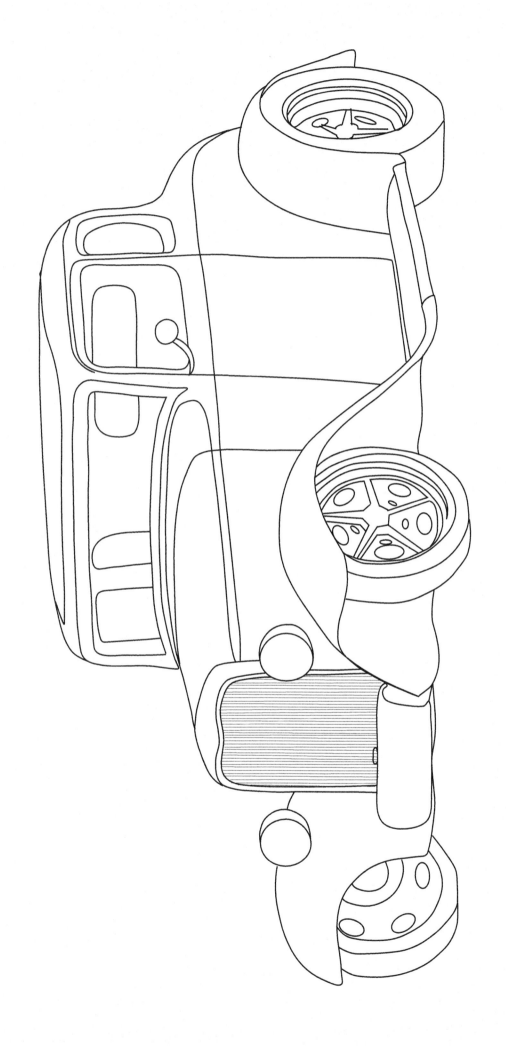

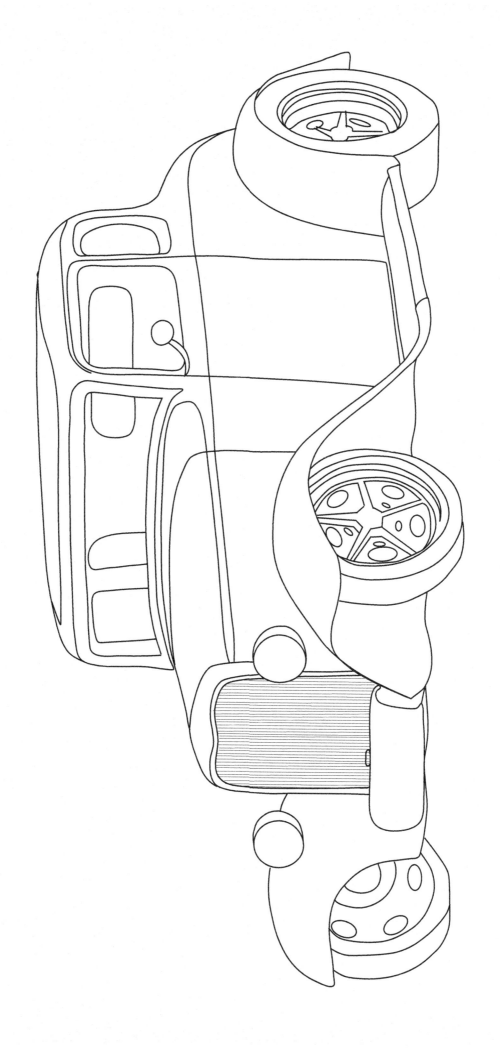

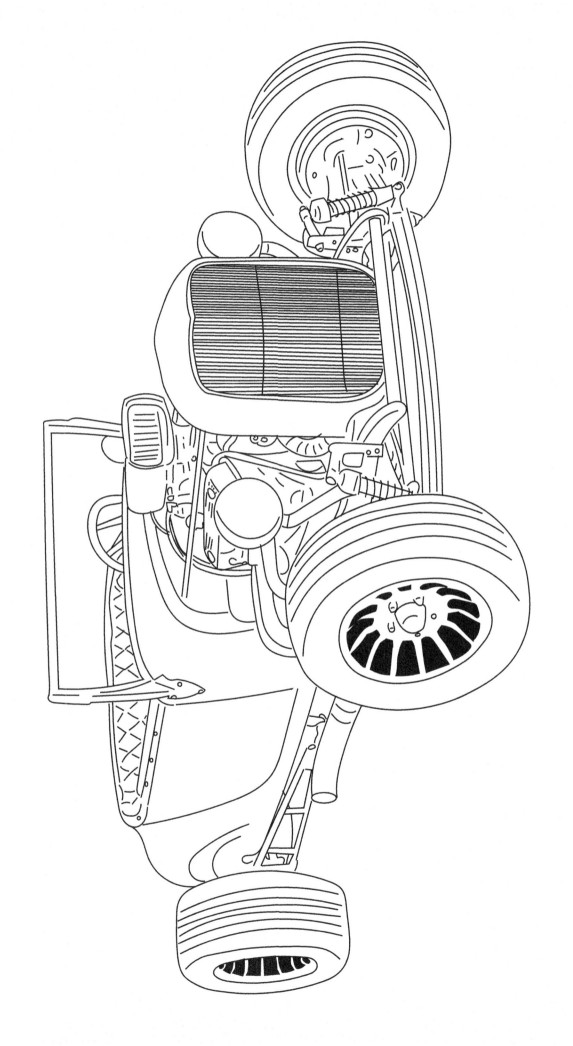

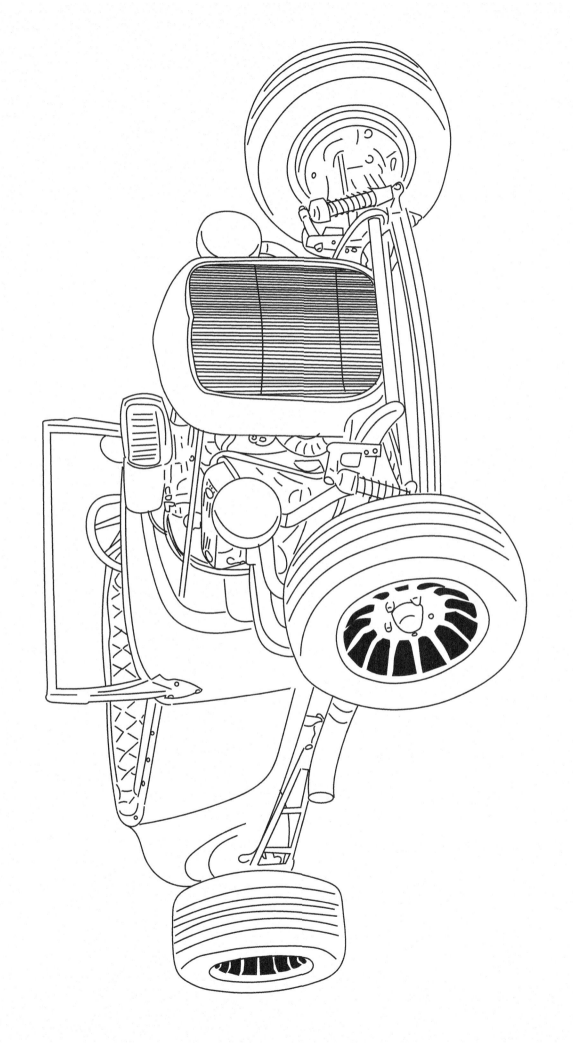

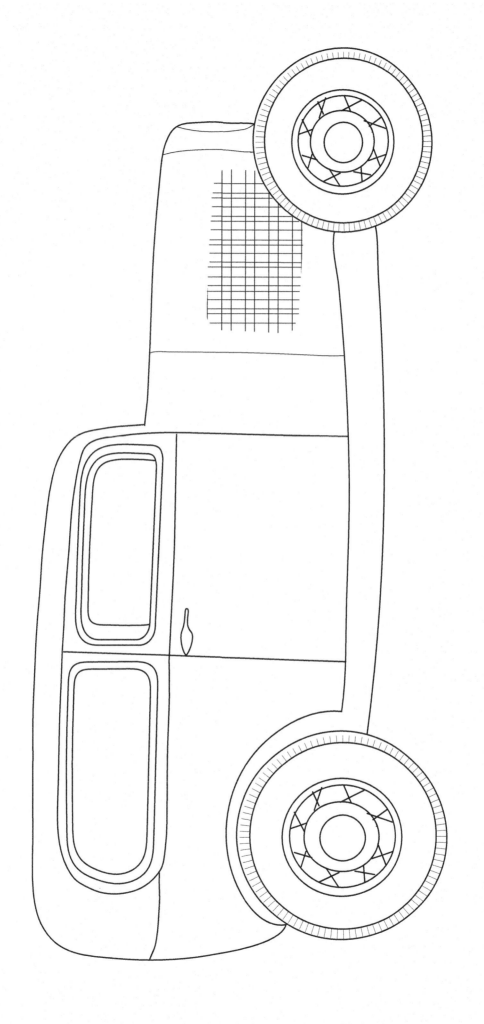

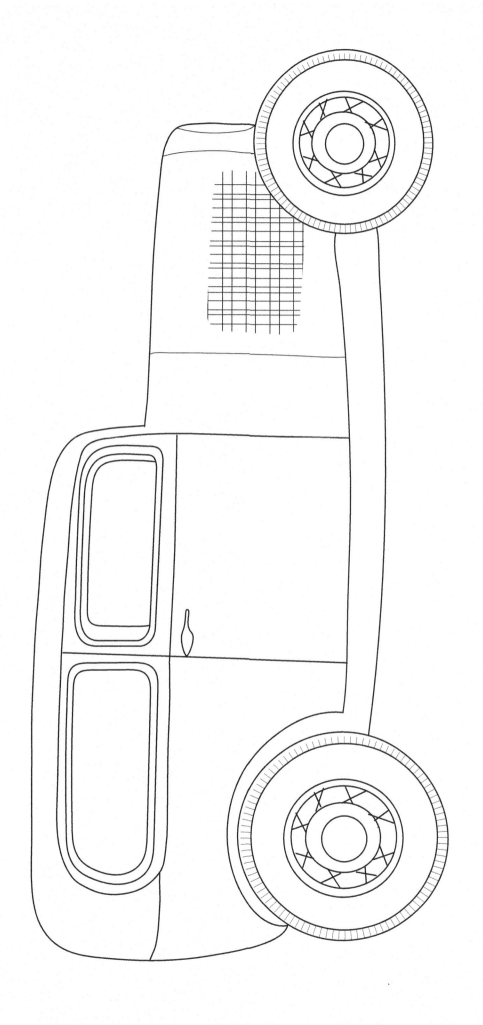

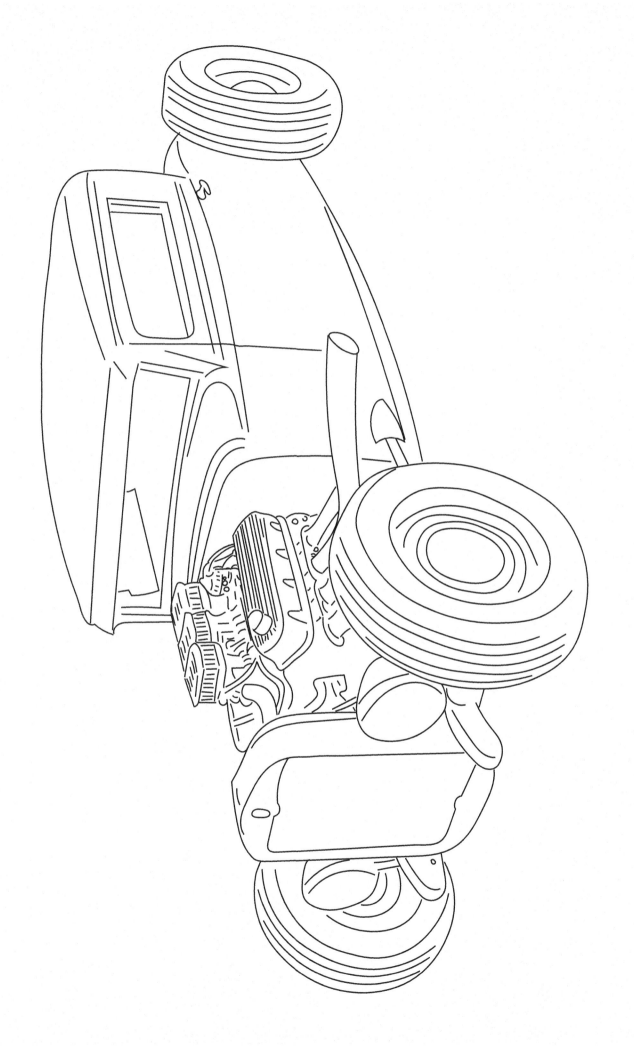

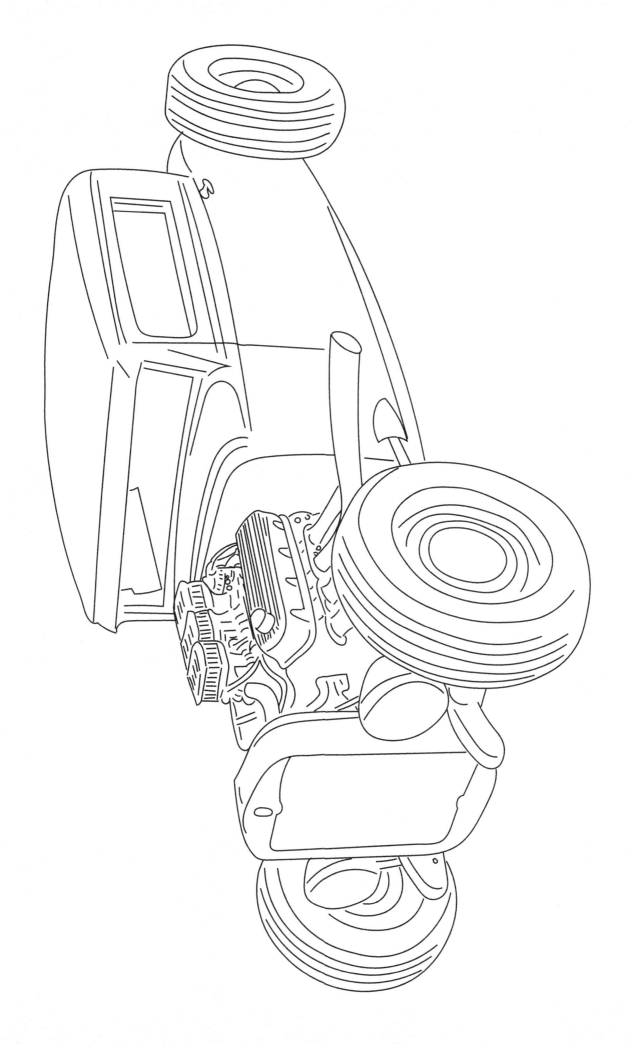

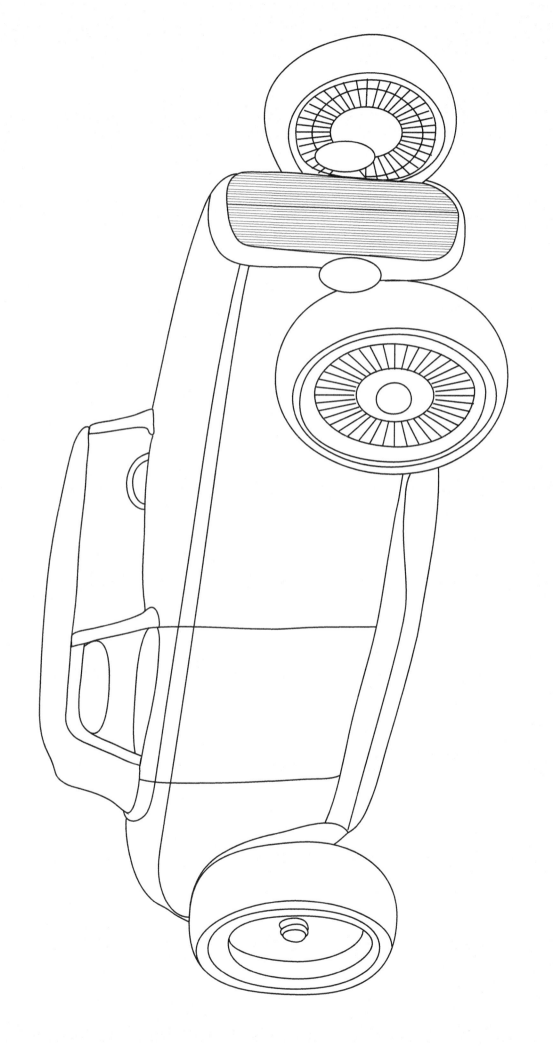

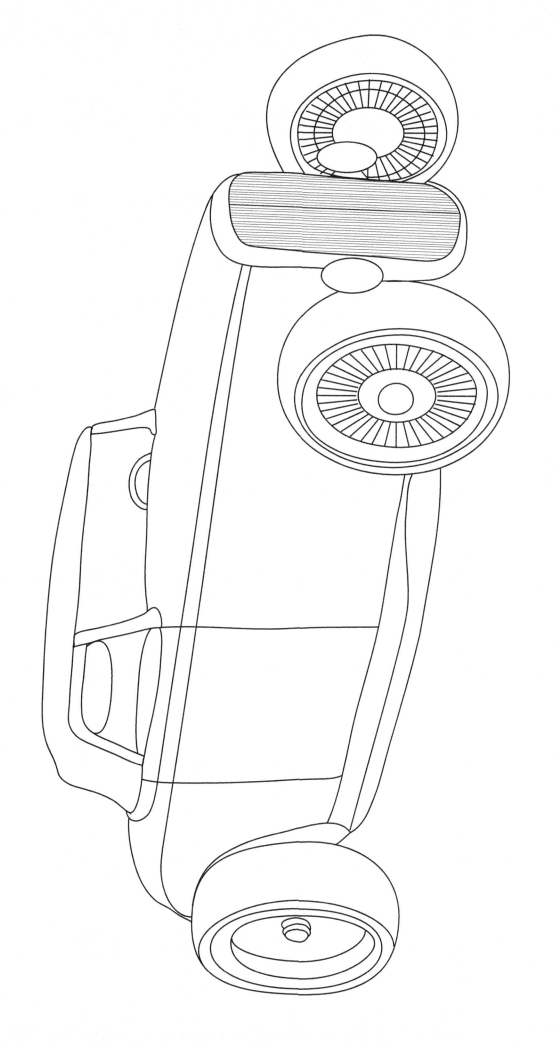

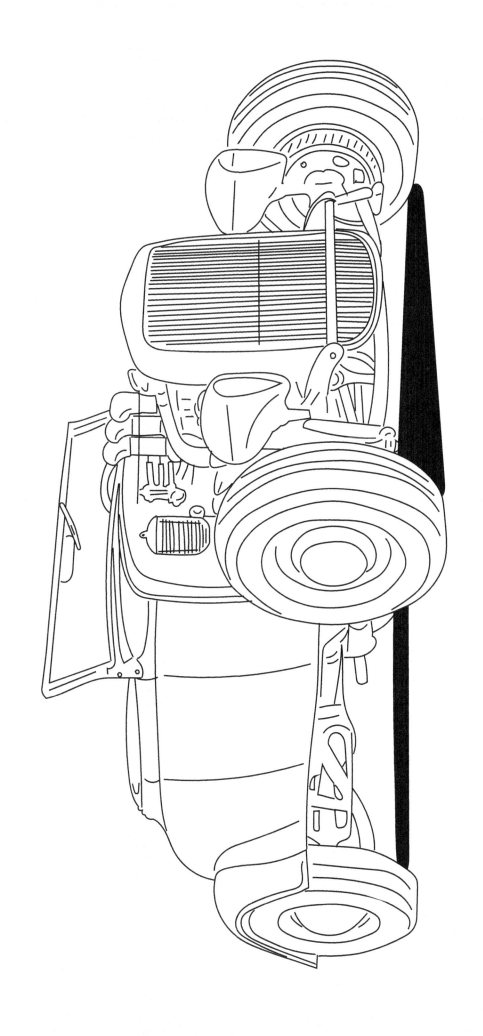

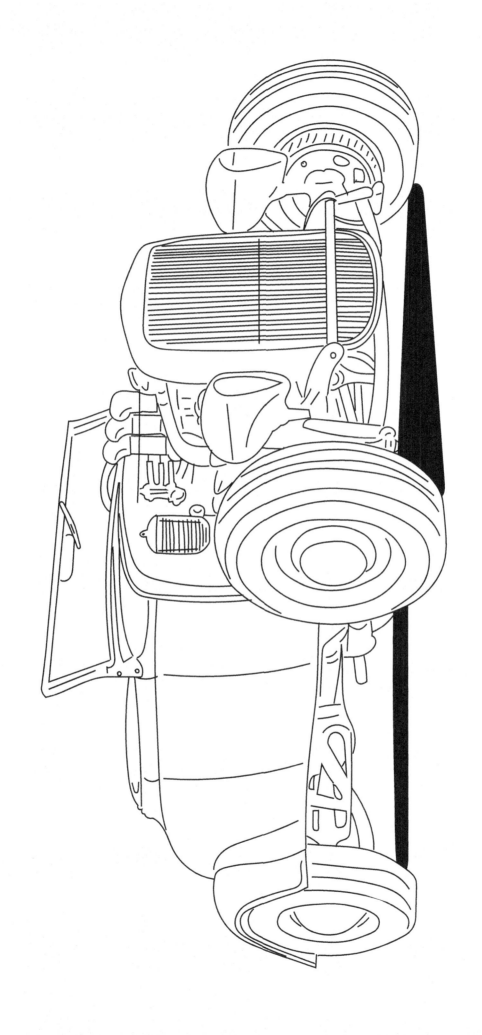

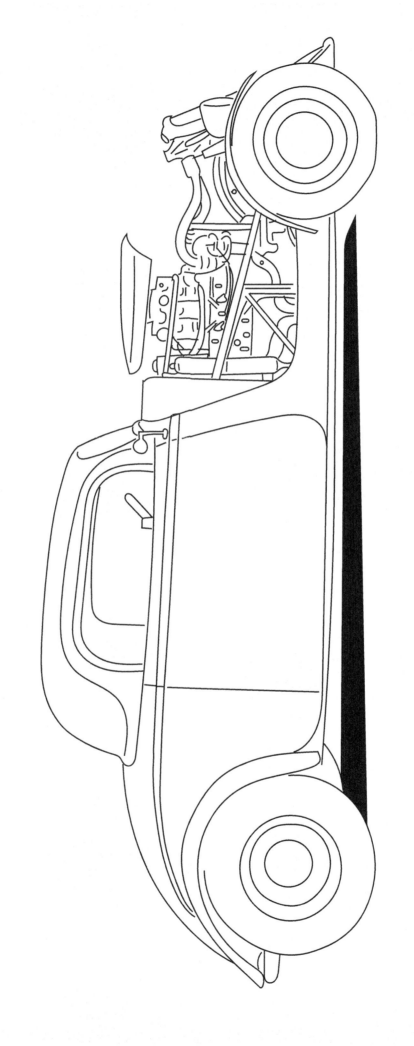

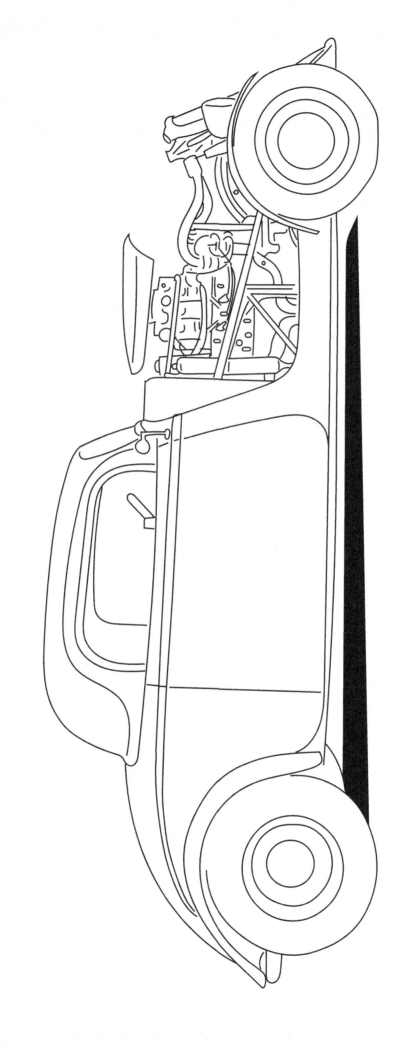

CPSIA information can be obtained
at www.ICGtesting.com
Printed in the USA
BVOW04s1304080118
504749BV00011B/94/P